The Best WEDDING SHOWER BOOK

A Complete Guide for Party Planners

COURTNEY COOKE

Meadowbrook Press

Distributed by Simon & Schuster
New York

Library of Congress Cataloging-in-Publication Data
Cooke, Courtney.
The best wedding shower book: a complete guide for party planners / Courtney Cooke.—Rev.
    p.   cm.
ISBN 0-88166-383-2 (Meadowbrook)—ISBN 0-671-31824-1 (Simon & Schuster)
1. Showers (Parties) 2. Weddings. 3. Entertaining. I. Title.
GV1472.7.S5 C67 2001
793.2—dc21   00-061296

Editorial Director: Christine Zuchora-Walske
Contributing Editor: Becky Long
Copyeditors: Kathleen Martin-James, Joseph Gredler, Megan McGinnis
Production Manager: Paul Woods
Graphic Design Manager: Tamara Peterson
Art Director: Peggy Bates
Illustrations: Joyce Shelton, Terri Moll

© 2003 by Meadowbrook Creations

Published by Meadowbrook Press, 5451 Smetana Drive, Minnetonka, MN 55343

www.meadowbrookpress.com

BOOK TRADE DISTRIBUTION by Simon & Schuster, a division of Simon and Schuster,
Inc., 1230 Avenue of the Americas, New York, NY 10020

06   10 9 8 7 6

Printed in the United States of America

Contents

Keeping the Party Rolling

Serving the Food

Buying the Gift

Appendix

Introduction

Your closest friend calls with exciting news. She's getting married! There are many details to discuss and, in the heat of the moment, you say you'd love to throw her a wedding shower. Then you hang up the phone—and panic sets in. You hate showers with their dumb games and endless small talk. You imagine your reputation for throwing great parties being destroyed. You, however, are stuck. You're the logical person to give the shower, and it's too late to back out. You ask yourself if it's possible to turn a tired old shower into a great party. You bet it is!

When you think about it, it's probably the trappings of the traditional shower that you dislike: silly games, fussy decorations, and fattening foods. In *The Best Wedding Shower Book,* you'll find tips to help you plan a fun, contemporary celebration that suits you, your guests, and the bride (and groom, if he's included). We've created a practical handbook that includes time- and money-saving hints for decorations and food. It also contains innovative gift ideas and exciting alternatives to outdated games. We've also included men in many of our shower plans—they participate in weddings, too—and we've provided ideas appropriate for celebrating second marriages.

Today's bride is dramatically different from her counterpart of thirty or forty years ago. She's often older, better educated, and may have been supporting herself for some time. She may already own many household necessities. In fact, she may have been married before or may have been living with the groom for several years. Even though the social circumstances surrounding showers have changed, the main reason for giving them has not. A shower is, above all, a celebration of the couple's decision to marry. It's an expression of emotional support and encouragement that combines gifts for the couple with good wishes and good advice.

So pack away your panic, dust off your "great party" reputation (or plan to start one), and read on. You're about to throw one heck of a party!

Planning a Shower

The idea of "showering" a bride with gifts began a long time ago in Holland. One version of a Dutch folktale tells of a wealthy young woman who fell in love with a poor miller. Her father forbade the marriage and denied the couple a dowry if they insisted on marrying. So the townspeople, sympathetic to this young couple, donated gifts to help them set up housekeeping.

Wedding showers eventually became popular with American "society women" by the early 1900s. These showers were often given as surprise parties. Women's magazines of the day described elaborate menus, decorations, and activities that included word games and puzzles popular at the time.

Today, women generally prefer a more casual approach to wedding showers. They enjoy a more relaxed setting where guests gather to celebrate the bride. Many hosts plan menus and activities that aren't even wedding related. Whatever you decide to do as host, be sure to plan. If you're organized, the party should run smoothly, allowing you and your guests time to relax and have fun.

Who Should Host the Shower?

Generally, someone other than an immediate family member gives the bridal shower. This person could be a close friend, an aunt, a cousin, or a member of the wedding party. Some people think it's in poor taste for the bride's mother or sister to give the shower, because the party then seems like a plea for gifts.

Setting the Date

The first thing you should do as host is set a date and time for the shower. Begin by asking the bride (and groom, if he's included) about available dates. Because her schedule will likely be hectic in the months prior to the wedding, consult her well in advance.

Most wedding showers are held a month or so before the big event. Throw a shower any closer to that date, and you're likely to have a harried bride on your hands. Remember that it's difficult for a bride to send shower thank-you notes promptly when attending to last-minute wedding details.

Also anticipate potential scheduling problems for your guests, particularly if your list includes people traveling long distances. Try to find a date and time that accommodates everyone.

Don't forget to check the calendar for major holidays or cultural events that may conflict with your shower date, such as Memorial Day weekend or the Super Bowl.

The Guest List

Prepare your guest list by talking to the bride first. She'll know who should or should not be invited. If you're planning a surprise party (rarely a good idea), the couple's parents or close friends will be happy to furnish you with a list of names, addresses, and phone numbers. Ask for this information well ahead of time.

If you know the bride through a club or organization, if you work with her, or if you have a group of mutual friends, you may already have a ready-made guest list, one in which the guests already know one another. Nevertheless, always consult the bride before finalizing the list.

A note about surprises: They're not recommended. A bride has many tasks on her plate in the months before the wedding—and little or no unscheduled time. You run the risk of planning a surprise shower that ends up conflicting with her wedding preparations (not a good idea). It's best to save the surprise for another party.

Choosing a Location

The location and availability of a given venue will influence your shower date and guest list, so think about the where well in advance. Also consider that while your home or apartment may be a convenient and inexpensive shower site for you, the location may be inconvenient for many of your guests, who may be forced to travel a long way for the party. If that's the case, consider a more central location.

While restaurants and clubs are obvious party spots, don't hesitate to try someplace different, such as a day spa, campground, boat, and so on. Try to find a place that will create the right ambiance for your celebration or that offers an activity your guests will enjoy.

Invitations

Depending on the style of your shower and the size of your guest list, you can choose to either send written invitations or invite people by phone. A written invitation ensures that important party details will be communicated accurately. It also serves as a nice keepsake for the wedding couple. (For tips on making your own invitations, see page 61.)

Be sure to include the following items on your written invitations: the date, time, and address (including directions) of the party; the bride's name (and groom's name, if necessary); your name, phone number, and address; gift registry information; RSVP information; and theme information. If you ask guests to RSVP, they're expected to notify you whether they'll be attending. If you write "Regrets only," guests are expected to respond only if they won't be attending. You should also give a deadline for the response. To get a good response, mail invitations at least three weeks before the shower date.

Dos and Don'ts

- **Do** plan ahead. Send your invitations at least three weeks before the shower date.
- **Do** take time before the shower to get organized so the party will run smoothly. This way, you'll have time to actually enjoy the shower.
- **Do** consider including men.
- **Don't** surprise the bride.
- **Do** have fun with decorations. Consider using decorations or centerpieces that incorporate household gadgets or linens, which can be given to the bride at the end of the party.
- **Do** include a bunch of balloons outside your door to greet guests.
- **Do** use your best linens and silver if you're planning a formal party.
- **Do** present foods attractively. Include garnishes.
- **Do** know the dietary restrictions of your guests when planning the menu. If you intend to serve meat, calorie-laden sweets, and alcoholic beverages, provide alternatives for those who can't or choose not to consume these items.
- **Do** serve foods that are easy to eat.
- **Don't** expect guests to balance a sit-down meal on their laps.
- **Do** seat one or two detail-minded persons near the bride to handle wrappings and record the gifts.
- **Do** consider humorous or fun gifts to help the bride relieve pre-wedding tension.
- **Do** remember to invite members of the wedding party and the mothers of the bride and groom.
- **Do** keep the shower short and sweet (usually two to three hours).
- **Do** consider using the wedding colors in your decorations.
- **Don't** play games that are embarrassing or awkward to guests.
- **Do** plan activities that guests will enjoy.
- **Do** select useful prizes for guests.
- Finally, **do** have a good time!

Checklist

You might find a checklist useful when planning your shower. Checking off completed tasks allows you to concentrate on other details. Also, if you plan to serve more than punch and munchies, write down your menu and post it in a handy spot in your kitchen. The reminder will be helpful as you prepare your shopping list. It'll also help you remember to serve that Caesar salad sitting in your refrigerator!

Two to Three Months before the Wedding
- ❑ Consult with the bride (and groom, if necessary) and select a date and time for the shower.
- ❑ Prepare a guest list.
- ❑ Choose a location and secure a venue.

One Month before the Shower
- ❑ Decide on a theme (optional).
- ❑ Make or buy invitations.

Three Weeks before the Shower
- ❑ Double-check the required postage for invitations.
- ❑ Have someone proofread the invitations for missing details or typos.
- ❑ Mail the invitations.
- ❑ Plan the menu.
- ❑ Plan the activities and prizes.
- ❑ Decide on your gift. (Allow more time if you plan to make your gift.)

One to Two Weeks before the Shower
❑ Make or buy decorations.
❑ Buy or complete your gift. (Wrap it now and avoid the last-minute rush!)
❑ Prepare your shopping list for menu ingredients.

One Week before the Shower
❑ Check that all appropriate serving dishes and utensils are on hand.
❑ Check that enough tables and chairs are on hand and in good condition.
❑ Wash and iron table linens if necessary.
❑ Check RSVPs to determine the number of guests.
❑ Call the bride to remind her of the shower.

Three Days before the Shower
❑ Buy all groceries except fresh bread and rolls.
❑ Order the centerpiece and other fresh flowers, if necessary.
❑ Clean the house.
❑ Check that all appropriate serving dishes and utensils are clean.
❑ Buy film, tapes, and batteries for the camera and video camera.
❑ Prepare the nametags and place cards.

The Day before the Shower
❑ Prepare as much of your menu as possible.
❑ Set the table and decorate the party room.
❑ Bring chairs and tables out of storage. Set up if possible.
❑ Assemble items that will be used for activities.
❑ Wrap the prizes.
❑ Make sure your gift is wrapped.

The Day of the Shower

- ❑ Arrange your centerpiece or pick it up at the flower shop.
- ❑ Buy fresh bread and rolls.
- ❑ Set out coasters (and ashtrays, if smoking will be permitted).
- ❑ Finish last-minute dusting and vacuuming.
- ❑ Prepare the rest of the menu.
- ❑ Set out a box and paper bag to store gifts and wrapping paper.
- ❑ Have a pen and paper ready for someone to record the gifts.
  (See the Shower Gift Record on page 62.)

Last-Minute Details

- ❑ Don't be surprised by an early arrival! Get dressed at least thirty minutes to an hour before guests are expected to arrive.
- ❑ Have coffee ready to brew and other beverages ready to serve.
- ❑ Greet your guests and have a good time!

Choosing a Theme

Incorporating a theme in your shower is optional, but it may help you coordinate the various aspects of your party. A theme can also make gift hunting easier for guests. If you know the bride will be enjoying several showers, you may want to narrow the scope of your party to provide her with gifts she won't be receiving elsewhere.

Simple themes work best, and we've outlined several options in the following pages. We've included creative suggestions for invitations, decorations, gift ideas, activities, and food. Keep in mind that you don't have to spend a lot of money. The best party details might be those you make yourself. As you read, consider how certain ideas might work independently of any particular theme, or mix and match various ideas to create your own theme.

"Oldies but Goodies" Showers

We've added a contemporary twist to each of these tried-and-true themes. If you're looking for tradition but don't want to compromise creativity, consider these shower options.

Kitchen Shower

Variations on the kitchen shower are virtually endless. You could incorporate gadgets, spices, recipes, a particular meal of the day, and so on.

Invitations

Write party details on a recipe card.

Decorations

Host the party in the kitchen if it's big enough. That's where folks usually end up anyway.

Gift Ideas

Request that each guest bring a spice along with her favorite recipe calling for that ingredient. Guests could also bring a serving dish or utensil used in preparing their recipes.

Activities

- As an icebreaker, put uncooked pasta shells into a jar and have guests guess the amount as they arrive at the party. The guest who comes closest to guessing the amount wins a prize. Be sure to count the shells in the jar before the party!
- Hold a contest in which guests identify a series of unlabeled spices by smelling, tasting, and looking at them. Award a prize to the guest who identifies the most spices.

- Hold an impromptu recipe contest in which each guest writes down her favorite recipe. Don't advertise the contest. Have guests try to write their recipes from memory. Gather the recipes in a keepsake book for the bride (after confirming their accuracy, of course).
- Stage a "Name That Gadget" contest by displaying a collection of uncommon kitchen tools. Award a prize to the guest who identifies the most items, and give the gadgets to the bride.

Variations on the Theme

- Host a "tasting" shower in which guests bring a gourmet dish, its recipe, and a necessary serving dish or utensil. For example, an Italian theme will generate both a delicious meal and wonderful gifts for the couple, such as a lasagna pan, breadbasket, salad bowls, and so on.
- Turn the shower into a winetasting. Ask your guests to bring two identical bottles of wine—one for tasting and one for giving. You provide the cheese and other munchies.
- Arrange for a consultant to do an in-home demonstration at your shower. The consultant can show guests how to make an entrée that will be served as the main dish. Guests could purchase the cookware that would first be used in the demonstration and then be given to the bride.

Basket Shower

A basket shower lets guests be creative in their gift selections. Inform guests that they should bring gifts that either are baskets or are in baskets.

Invitations

Write party details on a gift tag and attach it to a miniature basket. Add a headline that reads "A tisket, a tasket, it's time to fill a basket." Miniature baskets are available in craft and hobby stores. For a smaller guest list, tie party details to a small basket of flowers and have one delivered to each guest's doorstep.

Decorations
Use baskets in your decorating scheme. Display flowers in baskets.

Gift Ideas
Gifts could include a set of decorative nesting baskets, casserole dish with basket server, wastebasket, or painted basket filled with guest towels and decorative soaps. Give the bride a wicker laundry basket (or any large decorative basket) to store her gifts.

Food
Serve food items in baskets and place small baskets filled with snacks around the room.

Activities
- ❧ Advertise a prize for the most creative theme-gift presentation. Have guests vote for the winner, and award that guest a prize.
- ❧ Make a memory basket for the bride. Ask each guest to bring a household item that inspires a story about the bride. For example, the mother of the bride could bring a pair of scissors as a reminder of the time the bride cut off her sister's ponytail. Have each guest share her story with the group while placing her item in the basket. Make sure guests write their stories on gift cards.

Variation on the Theme
- ❧ Host a "box" shower and invite guests to bring anything that comes in a box.

Domestic Shower
A domestic shower is probably the least glamorous of all showers, but the buckets, brooms, mops, and other cleaning items the bride receives are no less needed. Receiving these items as gifts allows the bride to spend her money on other things. The hidden bonus is she'll never have to return a bucket because it's not the right color or size. With a little creativity, these gifts can be a lot of fun to open.

Invitations
Write party details on a pair of rubber gloves.

Decorations
Incorporate cleaning supplies in your decorating scheme. For added fun, have the bride wear a corsage made from small, inexpensive household items. Provide guests with snazzy rubber gloves embellished with lace glued around the cuffs and a fake gemstone glued onto the ring finger of the left glove. These gemstones are available in craft stores.

Gift Ideas
Build a gift "bride" from common household items. Use an ironing board for her body, a mop for her hair, and guests' gifts for anything else. Be creative! Don't forget to add a tulle veil and a bridal bouquet. Present the gift bride to the real bride during the gift opening.

Activities
- Ask each guest to write down her favorite cleaning tip and bring it to the shower along with the products needed to carry out the task. Share the tips during the party and store them in a keepsake book for the bride.
- As each guest arrives, give her five clothespins with one word written on each pin. You could write the groom's name, the word wedding, and so on. Guests aren't permitted to say these words during the party, and if a guest says one of these off-limits words, she must forfeit that clothespin to the guest who catches her saying it. The guest who collects the most clothespins by the end of the shower wins a prize.

Book Shower
This is the perfect shower for the bride who already owns most necessary household items. Ask each guest to bring the bride a book that's been the most useful in married life. The categories could include fiction, gardening, humor, cooking, remodeling, and so on.

Invitations

Design the invitation as a keepsake bookmark. It's easy to create on a computer. Consider laminating it to increase its longevity.

Decorations

Host the shower at a local bookstore. Find one that has a private meeting room, outdoor lunch area, or coffee shop. Ambiance will be abundant. Or ask the bookstore staff for old advertising posters to decorate your walls for a shower at home.

Gift Ideas

In addition to their favorite books, guests could bring related gifts, such as cookie cutters tied with ribbon to a cookbook or gardening gloves taped to a gardening book. Consider pooling funds with guests to buy a bookcase or some larger gift.

Activities

- Buy or make an address book for the bride and have guests fill in pertinent information like addresses, birthdays, anniversaries, phone numbers, and so on. This activity can be a great way for the bride to gather information about her new extended family and friends.
- Buy or make a scrapbook for the bride. Include instant photos, gift cards, nametags, and activities memorabilia. Have guests write best wishes and advice on separate pages. The bride can later include precious mementos from her wedding and the early days of married life.

China and Glassware Shower

Any bride who's registered for china and crystal patterns will welcome this shower.

Invitations

Attach party details to plastic stemware.

Decorations

Put tiny glass vases with fresh-cut flowers at each place setting. Invite guests to take them home as favors.

Gift Ideas

Let guests know where the bride is registered. If the pieces the couple has chosen are pricey, pool resources to buy a group gift. In addition to china and crystal, gift ideas can include kitchen glassware, dishes, vases, candleholders, and so on.

Activities

- Enjoy a winetasting using your finest crystal or glassware.
- Hire a florist to teach the group how to make a beautiful centerpiece. Send the demonstration centerpiece home with the bride.

Holiday or Seasonal Shower

This shower can be loads of fun while providing a wealth of unusual gifts the bride will enjoy for years to come. In a nutshell, guests choose or are assigned a holiday or season. Their task is to select an appropriate gift.

Invitations

Stuff party details inside a small Christmas stocking, plastic Easter egg, or Halloween treat bag.

Decorations

Follow the seasonal or holiday spirit when choosing colors, flowers, and other decorations.

Gift Ideas

On one hand, your task could become a shopping nightmare if the current date isn't in your assigned season. On the other hand, you could save lots of money if you're lucky enough to find a clearance section that contains items from your assigned holiday or season. Buy decorative pieces that reflect the season, or purchase a serving piece that complements the bride's china pattern (don't forget to include your favorite holiday recipe).

Activities

- Transform the gift opening into an entertaining story that imagines the newlyweds' first year. Assign each guest one of the holidays or seasons symbolized by the gifts. Make sure guests receive story assignments different from their gift assignments. Ask guests to take turns telling their stories about the bride and groom as gifts are opened. Because the stories and gifts will rarely correspond, the result will be hilarious.
- Go around the room and have each guest state her birth date or anniversary date (if she's married). Award a prize to the guest whose date comes closest to the couple's wedding date.

Romance Shower

This theme is designed to celebrate keeping romance alive after you are married.

Invitations

If valentines are in season, then look no further for invitations. If not, attach party details to something heart-shaped.

Decorations

Play soft, romantic music and decorate with lots of lighted candles. Use a heart-shaped ivy topiary for your centerpiece.

Gift Ideas

Think romantic (bottles of fine wine, wineglasses, CDs of sensual music, massage oil, sexy lingerie, and so on). For a group gift, plan a weekend getaway for the couple.

Food

Serve champagne with strawberries.

Activities

- ❧ Watch a romantic movie.
- ❧ Have guests share tips on how to keep romance alive in a relationship. Their gifts could correspond to the tips.

Time-of-Day Shower

This shower is based on a typical day in the life of the newlyweds.

Invitations

Write party details on a gift tag and attach it to a toy watch. Assign each guest a different time of day and suggest that she bring a gift corresponding to that time.

Decorations

Draw a clock face on the tablecloth. Use toy watches as napkin rings.

Gift Ideas

You might include a list of gift suggestions with the invitation. For example, an appropriate gift for 7:00 A.M. could be items that allow the couple to enjoy breakfast in bed. Send guests home with goodies like bubble bath or tea for bath time or bedtime.

Activities

❧ Accent the gift opening with clever stories about what a typical day might involve for the newlyweds. Have guests take turns prefacing each gift opening with a funny story appropriate for that time of day. Assign guests story times different from their gift times.

❧ Have each guest write a story to introduce her gift. Here's an example of an introduction that could be read before the 6:00 P.M. gift is opened: "It's six in the evening and [bride's name] is putting the final touches on her signature dish: macaroni and cheese. The doorbell rings and [groom's name] is relieved to find that there's someone to the rescue. Let's see who's at the door!" The bride then opens the six o'clock gift: a certificate for a free pizza.

❧ During the gift opening, set a timer to ring at various intervals. When the timer goes off, the guest whose gift is being opened wins a prize.

"The Party Is the Gift" Showers

Some showers can be planned around a specific activity so that the party itself is the gift. Many of the following ideas are particularly well suited to parties for the couple. Although decorations seldom befit this type of shower, we've included decoration ideas wherever appropriate.

Painting-Decorating-Gardening-Landscaping Shower

This shower gives guests the chance to help the bride and groom spruce up their house or apartment. Talk to the couple and determine what project they'd like help with. Then inform guests about the theme and encourage them to come dressed to work and to bring tools appropriate for the party (paint brushes, rollers, wallpapering tools, gardening tools, and so on).

Invitations
Write party details on a gift tag and attach it to a paintbrush, packet of garden seeds, or other appropriate item.

Gift Ideas
Expertise and elbow grease are the wonderful gifts given at this shower. However, you might also invite guests to purchase tools for the couple or to help pay for materials. Guests could also write their favorite painting or landscaping tips in a scrapbook for the couple.

Food
Enjoy a potluck meal. Coordinate the menu with guests to ensure variety, and don't forget to supply plates, cups, flatware, serving pieces, and so on.

Variation on the Theme

Stage separate showers for the bride and groom to occur concurrently. For example, the women could garden while the men paint the house.

Mail-Order Shower

If geographical or other circumstances prevent the bride and guests from gathering, consider hosting a mail-order shower. Include in each invitation a "refreshment" (gift certificate for a modest amount to a restaurant) and a "favor" (gift certificate for a modest amount to a bookstore, music store, and so on). Ask guests to mail both shower presents and photos of themselves "presenting" their gifts. The bride will enjoy a week of shower packages coming through the mail—surely the next best thing to being there!

Invitations

Glue a photo of the bride on the front, and don't forget to include "refreshments" and "favors."

Decorations

Invite guests to have a favorite photo of the bride enlarged to poster size. They could prop it on a chair to make it seem as if the bride were present.

Gift Ideas

Any shower gifts are appropriate, but they should be light and compact for shipping. Fragile items aren't recommended. You could encourage a certain type of gift based on a particular theme, such as kitchen items or linens, or you could simply recommend gifts that remind the bride of the giver, such as a pretty frame from a friend who is an avid photographer. Cash gifts mail well and are always a good fit.

Flea–Market Shower

This shower works well if the guests love garage sales and if you're able to hold the shower early in the morning. Give each guest a shopping bag and tell her to join the party at your house in an hour or two. When guests return, have each unpack her booty. The merchandise goes to the bride, of course.

Invitations
Design the invitation to look like a garage-sale ad, or write party details on a "Garage Sale" sign.

Gift Ideas
Guests may want to bring a wrapped gift to the shower in addition to their garage-sale purchases. Send guests home with pretty canvas shopping bags.

Food
Prepare a brunch that will be ready when the shoppers return.

Activities
Give prizes for the best bargain, the most useful gift, and the cleverest assortment.

Helping Shower

This party involves guests gathering to help the bride prepare for the wedding. Activities could include addressing invitations or decorating the reception hall. As host, try to choose an activity that can be completed by the number of guests invited in the time allotted.

Invitations
Include party details with something that symbolizes the party task. For example, if you'll be decorating the reception hall, write party details on a roll of crepe paper.

Gift Ideas

If guests still want to bring gifts, encourage them to bring items that will be helpful to the bride in some way. For example, a gift-wrap organizer can help the bride wrap presents for her sweetie more easily.

Food

If addressing wedding invitations will be an activity, serve the food after guests complete the task—just in case of spills.

Showers for the Couple and for Second Weddings

Emphasize romance when throwing these types of showers.

Honeymoon Shower

The look and feel of this shower can vary greatly, depending on the couple's honeymoon plans. It's best to follow the motto "When in Rome…" and pretend you're hosting the shower in the same place where the couple will be honeymooning.

Invitations

Try to get postcards of the honeymoon destination. Good resources include travel agents, chambers of commerce, and the Internet. Write party details on the postcards and mail to guests.

Decorations

Decorate with travel posters and brochures that depict the couple's honeymoon destination. Or create a more realistic look by using props and decorations that create the illusion of actually being there.

Gift Ideas

Sexy swimsuits and champagne would be perfect for a couple spending two weeks in Bermuda. Camping gear would be ideal for a couple heading to the mountains. Also, consider giving a group gift that includes a camera with film, certificates for free film processing, and a photo album.

Activities

- Plan activities relevant to the couple's honeymoon destination. For example, if the bridal pair is headed to Hawaii, host a luau and invite guests to dress the part. Play traditional music and serve ethnic foods.
- In an old suitcase, place a variety of items the bride should take on her honeymoon. Blindfold your guests and ask them to stick their hands into the suitcase and identify the items. The guest who identifies the most items wins a prize.

Variation on the Theme

If the couple is not planning to travel for their honeymoon, you could throw a "honeymoon at home" party. Gifts could include professional maid service, gift certificate to a romantic restaurant, and free baby-sitting (if the couple has children). Or guests could offer to cook the meal and do the housework themselves.

Bride-and-Groom Shower

Top hats and veils prevail at this event.

Invitations

Send party details attached to tiny bride-and-groom cake toppers.

Decorations

Dress dolls, bears, and other stuffed animals as brides and grooms. Add bride-and-groom cake toppers to individual desserts.

Gift Ideas

Ask female guests to bring gifts for the groom and male guests to bring gifts for the bride. As each gift is opened, the giver could explain how he or she thinks the gift will be used. Record these entertaining answers for posterity. (See the Keepsake Scrapbook on page 64.)

Activities

- Write a story about how the bride and groom met. When you're finished, delete key nouns, verbs, adjectives, and adverbs from the story. Ask guests to provide replacement words, but do not divulge the context in which the words appear. Read the resulting story to the group for guaranteed laughs.
- Cut out twelve full-length pictures of brides and grooms from bridal magazines. Cover the faces with cutouts of celebrities' heads. Number the pictures and pass them around the room. Challenge each guest to identify the famous brides and grooms by writing the names on a sheet of paper. Be sure to include a few less recognizable faces to make the game more interesting. For a humorous twist, glue a male celebrity's face onto a bride's body. Award movie passes to the guest who identifies the most celebrity brides and grooms.

"Roast the Couple" Shower

This party works best when the bride, groom, and guests have known one another for a long time. Each guest tells a humorous anecdote about the bride or groom and presents the couple with a gift related to the story. For example, a guest might say, "Bill was always getting into trouble at school for playing hooky and going fishing. Now he can play hooky with Marcia." The guest then hands the couple his-and-her fishing gear.

Invitations

Send party details attached to a baster or other roasting kitchen utensil.

Decorations

Use humorous memorabilia as decorations, such as baby photos of the bride and groom.

Gift Ideas

It's a good idea to coordinate gifts before the party (in case Bill's friends were all planning to tell the fishing story). Guests could also bring various barbecue items for the "roasting." A barbecue grill would make a perfect group gift.

Food

Since you're "grilling" your friends, you may as well fire up the barbecue and grill burgers, brats, whatever you like!

Activities

- If weather permits, play volleyball or some other group sport.
- Arrange for a hayride that ends with a marshmallow roast.

Entertainment Shower

This shower is perfect for the star-struck couple.

Invitations

Cut out a picture of a famous Hollywood couple from a magazine or newspaper. Cover the heads with those of the bride and groom. Glue the new couple onto a sheet of paper, and don't forget to add the funny caption and party details. Make copies and send.

Decorations

Have guests double as decorations by inviting them to dress as their favorite TV or movie stars.

Gift Ideas

Shower the bridal pair with gifts related to their favorite sources of entertainment: theater tickets, CDs, stereo equipment, and so on. For fun, try to secure autographed pictures of the bride and groom's favorite movie stars. Write letters to the celebrities several weeks before the party requesting a signed photo or letter mentioning the bridal pair. Keep a copy of each letter to read at the party. If the stars respond, read those letters at the party and give them to the bride and groom as keepsakes.

Food

Serve typical movie theater fare, such as popcorn, nachos, and candy. If you serve a more substantial meal, create fun menu names like "Clark Gable Potatoes" or "Hollywood Ham Sandwiches."

Activities

- ❧ If you want to provide entertainment that goes beyond gift opening and good conversation, consider renting a recently released video or a classic wedding movie, such as *Father of the Bride.*

- ❧ As guests arrive, give each a nametag with the name of a famous TV spouse (like Fred Flintstone or June Cleaver) written on it. Encourage guests to call one another by their celebrity names. After a time, have guests remove their nametags. Challenge guests to recall as many of the celebrity names as possible. The guest who remembers the most names wins a prize.

Hobby or Sports Shower

This shower highlights the bride and groom's favorite hobbies or sports.

Invitations

Send invitations attached to sporting items relevant to the party theme, such as fishing lures or toy sailboats.

Decorations

Decorate to complement your shower theme. For example, if the bride and groom enjoy camping, build a bonfire and have sleeping bags and lanterns double as decorations.

Gift Ideas

Give needed equipment for playing the chosen sport or hobby.

Activities

- ❧ Play the couple's favorite group sport or watch it on TV.
- ❧ Write the names of sports legends on slips of paper. Pin a slip onto each guest's back. Have guests determine their secret identities by asking one another yes-or-no questions. Award gold, silver, and bronze medals to the three fastest guests.

Anniversary Shower

This shower is based on traditional anniversary gifts (paper for the first year, tin for the tenth, silver for the twenty-fifth, and so on). Assign each guest an anniversary year and ask him or her to bring a gift associated with that anniversary. For example, the guest who is assigned the second anniversary (cotton) could bring matching sets of cotton pajamas.

Invitations

Tie two costume gold rings to a gift tag that features party details.

Decorations

Use anniversary-related party goods. Dust off those old family photos of wedding and anniversary celebrations.

Gift Ideas

See the Traditional Anniversary Gift List on page 66 to make assignments. Include a copy of this list with each invitation.

Activities

- Have guests vote for the most creative gift. Award a prize.
- Have the couple open the gifts in numerical order, starting with the first anniversary. Tell the couple what gift category is represented, and encourage them to guess the contents before opening the gift.

Family Showers

The following ideas are well suited to showers that primarily involve family.

Heirloom Shower

This shower salutes the bride's and groom's family histories.

Invitations

Glue a copy of an old family wedding photo onto the front of an invitation. Write party details on the inside.

Decorations

Decorate with borrowed family photos and other treasures.

Gift Ideas

Each guest should bring an existing family heirloom, such as an old butter dish, or an item destined to become a treasured heirloom, such as a handmade quilt or afghan.

Food

Serve family favorites. Send guests home with one of Grandma's famous cinnamon rolls and her secret recipe to make them.

Activities

❧ Encourage guests to tell stories that explain the significance of various family heirlooms (where they came from, how they were used, and so on).

❧ Tell guests you're going to play a memory game. Have the bride present a tray that contains several family heirlooms. After a few minutes, ask the bride to leave the room. Then ask the guests to write down as many details about the bride as they can remember, such as the color of her shoes, the jewelry she's wearing, and so on. The guest who recalls the most details wins a prize.

Variations on the Theme

❧ Craft a quilted heirloom for the newlyweds. Give each guest a quilt square to embroider, stencil, or appliqué. The squares can be completed before or during the party, depending on when you'd like to present the quilt to the couple.

❧ Host a "Words of Wisdom" shower in which family members are invited to share favorite household hints with the couple. Guests could also bring a corresponding gift. For example, someone with a clever suggestion for polishing silver could bring a silver chest or polishing cloths. Log these helpful hints in a keepsake scrapbook. (See page 64.)

Keeping the Party Rolling

Activities can be crucial to maintaining a high level of fun. If your guests aren't well acquainted, consider playing an icebreaker game to get people talking. If guests know one another well but haven't visited in a long time, you might limit game-playing time so guests can chat. Whatever you choose to do, remember to carefully match the activities with your guests' personalities. Well-planned party activities avoid a few common pitfalls, so keep in mind the following questions while you're brainstorming ideas:

- Will the activity encourage conversation? (Requiring guests to write answers to questions can, in some situations, suppress conversation. Also, writing answers while balancing cake and punch on your lap can be tricky.)
- Will the activities embarrass any of my guests?
- Are the games really fun? (To find out, ask yourself if you'd enjoy playing them at a nonshower party or talk to someone who's already tried the game.)

The following activities address these questions and virtually guarantee that your party will be a smashing success.

Icebreakers

Guess the Nametags
On each nametag, write the name of a famous person or draw a wedding-related object. As each guest arrives, attach her nametag to her back without letting her see what's on it. Remove mirrors from the room if possible. Instruct guests to ask one another yes-or-no questions to determine their secret identities. Award a prize to the guest who needs the fewest number of questions. This game gets people talking right away and helps them learn one another's real names.

General Advice
After all your guests have arrived, ask them to introduce themselves and relate their best advice for a happy marriage. Or select other topics, like where they would go on their dream honeymoon and why. Record these pearls of wisdom for the bride. (See the Keepsake Scrapbook on page 64.)

What's the Bride Wearing?
Allow your guests to visit for a while, then signal the bride to leave the room. Next, ask your guests to write answers to questions about the bride. What color are her shoes? Is she wearing a skirt or slacks? Is she wearing earrings? Include questions about the bride's personal interests. Award a prize to the guest with the most correct answers. (Explain this activity to the bride in advance, so she can screen the questions and provide correct answers.)

Singing Telegram
During the party, have guests as a group make up lyrics to "Here Comes the Bride" or some other wedding tune. When guests are ready, have them serenade

the bride. Or ask each guest to write her own lyrics before the party. Each could then sing her version to the bride at the shower. (Make sure your guests will be okay with singing in public.) Gather all the made-up lyrics as keepsakes for the bride. Also, consider videotaping the concert.

Keeping Romance in the Marriage

Ask guests to take turns telling their favorite hints for keeping a marriage exciting. Record this advice on a cassette tape or in a scrapbook for the bride. (See the scrapbook activity on page 14.)

Lovers' Lane

Guests take turns reminiscing about favorite romantic spots and relating their funniest tales about falling in love.

Games and Activities

Best Wishes

Provide note cards for guests to write helpful and humorous advice for specific marital events. You might include the couple's wedding night, first anniversary, day after their first fight, and so on. Write the event names on envelopes and place the note cards inside. Have the bride read the cards at the party, or ask her to read the appropriate card on the day of the event.

Complete the Quotation

Read the first half of each quotation on page 67. Ask guests to write down the rest of the quotation or have them make up a humorous ending. Award prizes to the smartest and funniest writers.

Famous Pairs

Before the party, create a list of famous pairs of lovers such as Rhett and Scarlett. Divide guests into two teams. Have the first member of Team 1 read the name of a famous lover, then ask the first member of Team 2 to identify the corresponding partner. Use a timer, if you like. If he or she doesn't know the answer, the second member of Team 1 gets a chance. Go back and forth between the teams until someone answers correctly. Teams get a point for each correct answer. Continue until all the pairs have been identified. The team with the most points wins a prize.

The Name Game

Have each guest write the bride's and groom's first names on a piece of paper. (Include their last names if both have short first names.) Have guests try to form the most words from the letters found in the names within an allotted time. Award prizes for the highest total and the funniest words.

Love Drawings

Before the party, write down several words and phrases having to do with love and marriage on slips of paper and place them in a basket. One at a time, have each guest draw a slip and then draw clues about it on a chalkboard or other erasable surface. The other guests try to figure out what the clues represent. The guest who guesses correctly gets a point, and the guest with the most points wins a prize. Consider setting a time limit for guessing each item to keep things moving.

Roast

Have guests take turns telling true stories about the couple. Encourage funny, occasionally outrageous, but always tasteful recollections. The longer the guests have known the couple, the funnier the stories are likely to be. (See "Roast the Couple" Shower on page 24.)

Toast

Have guests take turns toasting the bride and groom. Use a tape recorder or camcorder to capture the action.

This Is Your Life

Pattern your shower after the TV show *This Is Your Life*. (This game requires a bit more preparation, but it'll be worth every ounce of effort.) First, present a slide show or home movie of the bride and groom when they were young. Have a mystery guest waiting in the wings while the video is playing. Ask a guest to narrate what's happening on screen from the mystery guest's perspective. When the presentation ends, ask the bride (and groom, if he's included) to identify the person who is talking about them, then have that person join the party. This is especially fun if you can find an unexpected acquaintance (like a former teacher) to be the mystery guest.

The Firstborn Profile

Have guests help you predict the attributes of the couple's first child, but don't let them know they're doing so! As each guest arrives, choose a category from the The Firstborn Profile on page 68 and ask him or her to give you an appropriate word to fill in the blank. Guests unknowingly choose the baby's sex, first name, middle name, hair color, eye color, and so on. For the height blank, limit the possibilities to numbers between fifty-four and eighty-four. Limit the weight options to numbers between ninety-five and three hundred. Add more categories, if necessary, so that each guest provides one attribute. When the future baby's profile is finished, your guests will enjoy hearing that the couple's first child will be a six-foot-tall female sumo wrestler with lavender eyes and cinnamon-colored hair, weighing only 103 pounds! Make sure to give the profile to the bride and groom.

Scavenger Hunt

This shower works well if you plan to take your party on the road. (Don't forget the designated driver.) Several hours before the party, stash small gifts in the bars and nightspots you'll be visiting. Be sure to get permission from the owners or managers first. When you get together for your night on the town, present the bride with a list of places where she might find presents. If you want to be really devilish, hide something in the men's room of a busy bar.

Name That Wedding Tune

Divide guests into two teams. Have teams identify the titles of traditional wedding songs and popular love songs as they're played. This game could be really fun if a guest plays the piano. The team with most correct answers wins a prize.

Thank-You Drawing

Have guests write their names and mailing addresses on thank-you-note envelopes. Place the envelopes in a basket for a prize drawing. The bride can then mail her thank-you notes in the addressed envelopes.

Unstructured Activities

Who says you need structured activities? Sometimes, good friends need only good food, comfortable surroundings, and stimulating conversation to have a good time. If the chatter lags, throw in one of the following conversation starters:

- What's the funniest thing that ever happened at a wedding you attended?
- What went wrong on your honeymoon?
- What's the most frustrating part of being married?
- What's the best or worst advice for the newlyweds?
- What went wrong on your wedding night?
- How have weddings and marital roles changed over the years?
- What pet names have you used for your spouse? What ones have you heard about or would like to use someday?

Prizes

Choose prizes that are both useful and memorable, always keeping your guest list in mind. Since you have no idea who will win which prize, stick with generally well-received items. Consider spending a little more on a few nice prizes rather than buying a lot of cheap ones. Remember, tastes can vary dramatically, even among close friends. And it's a good idea to have a few spare prizes on hand in the event of a tie. The following list will get you started:

- Stationery
- Mugs
- Small potted plants
- Refrigerator magnets
- Heart-shaped ice cube trays
- Fancy soaps
- Guest towels
- Six-pack of beer or bottle of wine
- Office supplies
- Fishing lures
- Gift-wrapping
- Votive candles
- Travel-size toiletries
- Postage stamps
- Potpourri
- Film
- Batteries
- Fun note pads or message pads
- Candy
- Bubble bath
- Napkin rings
- Coasters
- Hand lotion
- Pretty paper napkins and plates
- Mixed nuts or snack foods
- Golf tees
- Tennis balls

For more ideas, browse in dollar stores, gift shops, or the notions sections of department stores.

Serving the Food

Good food is the common denominator for most successful parties. Wedding showers are no exception. Don't limit yourself to the old standbys—sweet desserts and coffee—or the predictable casserole-sweet roll-Jell-O medley. Instead, serve foods you would enjoy at a party.

When planning the menu, first consider when the party will take place. The most popular times for showers are weekend afternoons and weekday evenings. Of these, only weekend afternoons require full meals. For other times you can serve a variety of snacks and desserts.

Your next consideration is the guest list. If you're serving thirty or forty people, choose foods that don't require much fuss. Offer beverages that are prepared in quantity and served from a punch bowl or pitcher. No matter how many people are coming, choose recipes that can be prepared ahead of time so you can get out of the kitchen and into the fun when the party starts.

If your group is too large to sit comfortably at your kitchen or dining room table, don't serve a meal that requires a knife. Balancing a plate on a lap while cutting meat or buttering a roll is difficult to manage gracefully and invites disaster. Instead, set out platters of finger foods or snack-size versions of your favorite dishes. Finger foods can be just as nutritious as any casserole. In fact, you can serve a fully balanced meal in snack-size portions. This approach offers additional advantages:

- ❧ Conversations will not be interrupted by a sit-down meal.
- ❧ Guests are free to fill their plates when they're hungry and can move around to find a comfortable spot to eat.
- ❧ Guests don't feel obliged to eat a full meal.

Be sure to anticipate special dietary restrictions your guests may have, and offer plenty of low-calorie options.

Recipes

Hors d'Oeuvres and Snacks

Appetizers and snacks are popular party foods, and they're particularly welcome at showers. Serve a generous selection of these tasty morsels at either an afternoon or an evening shower. Experiment with your favorite recipes for sandwiches, salads, and so on to adapt them for snacking. (You might need to decrease certain baking times.) Snack-size tidbits are tastier and more nutritious than chips and dips.

Caution: Don't plan to serve any experiments you haven't tasted (and loved). Prepare the food far enough in advance to find out what works. Otherwise, you might be making an unexpected trip to the deli.

Here a few ideas for jazzing up your presentations:

- ❧ Cut desserts, cakes, and gelatin salads in advance and place them in cupcake liners, or bake single servings directly in the liners. If you have access to plastic wedding cake tiers, try arranging cupcakes, petits fours, or other individual desserts on the tiers to resemble a wedding cake.
- ❧ Present your favorite casserole or salad in a single-serving "nest" made from one of these items:

- Pastry shell: Buy preformed pastry shells at a bakery, or buy frozen dough and shape them yourself.
- Toast cup: Press bread slices into a muffin tin and toast them in the oven until firm and golden.
- Potato bird's nest: Buy ready-made or make them yourself. You'll need a special tool to hold the shredded potatoes in form while you fry the nests.

❧ Make finger Jell-O in a variety of shapes and colors. (See page 43 for the recipe.) Although it's usually recommended for toddlers, finger Jell-O is attractive, tasty, and fun to eat. Make the Jell-O more decorative and convenient to handle by setting each piece in a candy liner. Garnish with a squirt of mayonnaise or whipped cream.

❧ Make finger sandwiches using small slices of cocktail rye or quarter slices of white bread. Or ask your baker to slice the loaf lengthwise. Then cut the slices into shapes with cookie cutters. Spread filling on top before removing the excess bread. Garnish the cutouts and arrange them on a platter. Add folded, thinly sliced cheese and cold meats to the platter. For a complete mini-meal, complement the sandwich platter with a tray of deviled eggs, olives, pickles, and vegetable sticks.

The following is a list of popular snack recipes:

Baby Burritos

Cheese, grated	*Beef or chicken (cooked),*
Onion, grated	*shredded or diced*
Tomato, chopped	*Tortillas*
Lettuce, shredded	*Sauces for dipping (guacamole, sour*
Black olives, sliced	*cream, salsa, and so on)*

Cut tortillas into quarters and top them with a combination of the above items or add your own. Roll into tiny burritos. Garnish with sliced olives. Serve with a variety of dipping sauces.

Taco Dip

7¾-ounce can guacamole dip,
   thawed, frozen, or refrigerated
1½ cups tomatoes, chopped
1½ cups lettuce, chopped
2 tablespoons onion, chopped
1½ cups cheddar cheese, shredded

Spread and sprinkle ingredients on a tray in the order listed. Serve with taco chips. Serves 6–8.

Enchiladas

10–12 flour tortillas
2 cans cream-of-chicken soup
1 pint sour cream
4-ounce can mild green chilies,
   chopped
2 cups cheddar cheese, grated
1½ pounds ground beef,
   browned and drained
1 pouch taco seasoning
Ripe olives, sliced
Vegetable oil

Preheat oven to 400°F. Mix taco seasoning with ground beef, adding water according to package instructions. In separate bowl, mix soup, sour cream, and chilies. Add half this mixture to beef mixture. Dip each side of tortillas in small amount of vegetable oil. Place beef and cheese on tortillas, reserving half the cheese. Roll up tortillas and place them seam-side down in ungreased 9-by-13-inch pan. Pour remaining sauce over top. Cover with remaining cheese and sliced olives. Bake 30 minutes. Serves 10–12.

Cucumber Sandwiches

2–3 cucumbers
8 ounces cream cheese, softened
1 loaf white or rye bread, thinly sliced

Cut bread into circles using cookie cutter or opened tin can. Spread cream cheese on bread. Top with thin slice of cucumber. Serve chilled.

Water Chestnut Wraparounds

Two 8-ounce cans whole water
   chestnuts, drained
¼ cup soy sauce

2 tablespoons sugar
10 bacon slices

Preheat oven to 350°F. Cut water chestnuts in half and marinate in mixture of soy sauce and sugar at least 30 minutes. Cut bacon slices in thirds and wrap around water chestnuts. Secure with toothpicks. Bake on broiler pan or in shallow pan until bacon is crisp. Makes 30.

Cheddar and Bacon Cracker Spread

1 cup cheddar cheese, shredded
¼ cup parsley, chopped
2 tablespoons green onions, sliced

½ cup margarine
¼ cup cooked bacon, crumbled

Combine ingredients in small mixing bowl. Beat at medium speed until well mixed, scraping bowl often. Refrigerate 2 hours before serving. Makes 1¼ cups.

Magic Finger Jell-O

2 envelopes unflavored gelatin
2½ cups water

6-ounce package Jell-O

Dissolve unflavored gelatin in 1 cup cold water. Set aside. In saucepan, bring 1 cup water to boil and add Jell-O. Return to boil and remove from heat. Add gelatin mixture. Stir and add ½ cup cold water. Pour into lightly greased pan and refrigerate until solid (about 2 hours). Cut into squares and store in airtight container in refrigerator.

Luncheons and Brunches

Because afternoons are popular times to entertain, luncheons and brunches are popular shower ideas. Several types of foods are appropriate, including egg dishes, casseroles, sandwiches, fruit salads, soups, and poultry or seafood salads.

You can be creative without having to fuss. One fun, easy approach to an afternoon shower is a salad potluck. Guests bring their favorite salads or chopped salad ingredients. You provide a variety of dressings, rolls, beverages, and desserts. Arrange everything on a buffet and allow guests to build their own salads.

Remember, prepare as many dishes as possible ahead of time so you're free to enjoy the shower. Good food is important, but it's not the main reason for the party.

Cheese-Onion Pie

1½ cups fine cracker crumbs
   (approximately 40 crackers)
⅓ cup butter or margarine, melted
3 cups onions, thinly sliced
   (3 large onions)
2 tablespoons butter

1 cup milk
3 eggs, slightly beaten
1 teaspoon salt
¼ teaspoon pepper
2 cups cheddar cheese, shredded

Preheat oven to 350°F. Combine crumbs and melted butter and press evenly into 9-inch pie pan. Brown onions in remaining butter and place on crust. Scald milk and add slowly to beaten eggs, stirring constantly. Add salt, pepper, and cheese to mixture and pour over onions. Bake 30–40 minutes (until knife inserted in center comes out clean). Serves 6–8.

Open-Face Turkey Sandwiches

2 cups cooked turkey breast, diced
8-ounce can unsweetened
   pineapple chunks, drained
¾ cup celery, diced
¾ cup apple, chopped
⅓ cup mayonnaise
¼ teaspoon white pepper
¼ teaspoon curry powder
6 bread slices
2 tablespoons mayonnaise
6 lettuce leaves, crisp

Combine first 7 ingredients and stir until well mixed. Cover and refrigerate at least 2 hours. Toast bread, if desired. Spread remaining mayonnaise on bread or toast and top with lettuce. Spoon turkey mixture evenly onto each sandwich. Makes 6 sandwiches.

Pasta Salad

8 ounces tortellini shells
1 small onion, chopped
1 can water chestnuts, drained and sliced
¼ cup red wine vinegar
¼ green pepper, chopped

Cook tortellini shells according to package instructions. Drain and cool. Combine all ingredients. Chill and marinate at least 3 hours before serving.

Chinese Chicken Salad

2 cups cooked chicken or turkey, diced
2 stalks celery, chopped (1 cup)
8½-ounce can water chestnuts,
2 green onions, thinly sliced
   drained and sliced
Two 2-ounce cans pimientos,
   diced and drained
10-ounce can bamboo shoots, drained
¾ cup mayonnaise
2 tablespoons soy sauce
1 tablespoon lemon juice

Combine chicken and vegetables. Toss and chill. In separate bowl, stir together mayonnaise, soy sauce, and lemon juice. Chill. Combine both mixtures and toss before serving. Serves 4–6.

Hot Seafood Salad

1 pound crabmeat

2 cups celery, chopped

1 can mushrooms, drained

2 ounces almonds, slivered or sliced

1 pint mayonnaise (not salad dressing)

Bread crumbs, buttered

2 cans shrimp or 1 pound fresh shrimp

1 green pepper, chopped

8-ounce can water chestnuts, sliced

1 medium onion, chopped

2 teaspoons Worcestershire sauce

Mix all ingredients except bread crumbs 24 hours before serving. Cover and refrigerate. Preheat oven to 400°F. Top mixture with buttered bread crumbs and bake 30 minutes. Serves 8–10.

Chicken Broccoli Hotdish

30 ounces broccoli spears, cooked crisp-tender

4½ cups chicken, broken into pieces (4 breasts)

Two 10-ounce cans cream-of-chicken soup

1 cup mayonnaise

1 teaspoon curry powder mixed in 2 teaspoons butter

1 cup cheddar cheese, grated

¾ cup buttered bread crumbs or crushed potato chips

Preheat oven to 350°F. Alternate layering broccoli and chicken in greased 9-by-13-inch pan. Mix other ingredients, except crumbs or chips, and pour over top. Spread crumbs or chips over top. Bake 30–45 minutes. Serves 8–10.

Tip: Assemble in advance and bake just before serving.

Desserts

If you're entertaining in the afternoon or evening, consider serving a selection of dessert coffees, fancy teas, and liqueurs. Then bring on the cookies, bars, and candies—or throw an all-out chocolate extravaganza! However, don't neglect your guests who are trying to cut back on calories or avoid caffeine. Include a fresh fruit plate and at least one caffeine-free beverage. Consider arranging the cookies, bars, or small cakes on plastic wedding cake tiers.

Poppy Seed Coffee Cake

18-ounce package yellow
  cake mix
3-ounce package coconut
  instant pudding mix

4 eggs
1 cup hot water
½ cup vegetable oil
¼ cup poppy seeds

Preheat oven to 350°F. Grease and flour 10-inch Bundt or tube pan. Combine ingredients in large mixing bowl and blend. Beat 4 minutes at medium speed. Pour batter into pan and bake 50 minutes. Serve warm or cold. Serves 12–18.

Sour Cream Coffee Cake

Batter:
  ½ cup butter or margarine, softened
  ½ cup shortening
  1 cup sugar
  2 eggs
  2 cups all-purpose flour
  1 teaspoon soda
  ½ teaspoon salt
  1 cup sour cream
  1 teaspoon vanilla

Topping:
  ½ cup granulated sugar
  ⅓ cup brown sugar, packed
  1 teaspoon cinnamon
  1 cup pecans, chopped

Preheat oven to 350°F. Grease 9-by-13-inch pan. Cream butter, shortening, and sugar. Beat in eggs. In bowl, combine flour, soda, and salt. In small bowl, combine sour cream and vanilla. Alternate adding flour mixture and sour cream mixture to butter mixture. Pour half of batter into pan. Mix topping ingredients in small bowl. Sprinkle half of mixture over batter in pan. Spoon remaining batter over topping, spreading lightly to cover. Sprinkle remaining topping over batter. Bake 30–35 minutes. Serve warm or cold. Serves 12–20.

French Silk Pie

9-inch baked pie shell or graham
　cracker crust
¾ cup butter, softened
1 cup sugar
1 teaspoon vanilla

3 eggs
3 ounces unsweetened chocolate,
　melted and cooled
Whipped cream
Almonds

Blend butter and sugar in mixing bowl. Add vanilla. Add eggs one at a time, beating well after each. Blend in chocolate. Pour batter into pie shell and chill at least 1 hour before serving. Garnish with whipped cream and almonds. Keep refrigerated.

　　Caution: Uncooked eggs can contain salmonella bacteria. Consider using pasteurized eggs or an egg substitute.

Pink Lemonade Ice Cream Pie

¾ cup gingersnap crumbs
⅔ cup graham cracker crumbs
　(about 8 crackers)
1 tablespoon sugar
¼ cup butter or margarine, melted

1 quart vanilla ice cream, softened
6-ounce can frozen pink lemonade
　concentrate, thawed
Lemon slices and/or mint leaves

Preheat oven to 350°F. In bowl, combine crumbs, sugar, and butter. Press mixture firmly onto bottom and sides of 8- or 9-inch pie pan. Bake 10 minutes and cool. Combine ice cream and lemonade. Mix well and pour into crust. Freeze until firm. Garnish with thin lemon slices and/or mint leaves. Serve frozen or slightly thawed.

Pumpkin Ice Cream Pie

9-inch graham cracker crust
¼ cup brown sugar, packed
¾ cup canned pumpkin
½ teaspoon cinnamon
¼ teaspoon ginger
Dash nutmeg

Dash cloves
¼ teaspoon salt
1 quart vanilla ice cream
½ cup walnuts, chopped
Whipped cream and/or nutmeg

Combine brown sugar, pumpkin, spices, and salt in small saucepan. Boil 30 seconds, stirring constantly. Cool thoroughly. Scoop ice cream into mixing bowl and add pumpkin mixture. Blend. (Do not allow ice cream to melt.) Fold in walnuts. Pour mixture into crust and freeze until firm. Garnish with whipped cream and sprinkle with nutmeg, if desired.

Cashew Caramel Yummies

Batter:
　½ cup salted cashews, chopped
　2 eggs, slightly beaten
　¾ cup all-purpose flour
　½ cup brown sugar
　½ teaspoon baking powder
　½ cup granulated sugar
　¼ teaspoon salt

Topping:
　¼ cup brown sugar, packed
　2 tablespoons butter or
　　margarine, softened
　1½ tablespoons cream
　⅓ cup salted cashews

Preheat oven to 350°F. Combine first 3 batter ingredients. Stir in ½ cup cashews. In separate bowl, combine next 3 batter ingredients and stir into egg mixture. Pour mixture into greased 9-inch-square pan. Bake 20–25 minutes. Combine topping ingredients. Remove pan from oven and spread topping mixture over top. Broil 1–3 minutes or until bubbly. Cool and cut into bars. Makes 20–24 bars.

Cinnamon and Sugar Snack Bread

1 loaf frozen white bread dough, thawed	½ cup sugar
½ stick butter or margarine, softened	1 teaspoon cinnamon, to taste
	½ cup almonds, sliced

Preheat oven to 375°F. Press bread dough into greased 9-by-13-inch pan. Allow dough to rise for several hours. Spread butter or margarine on top. In separate bowl, combine sugar and cinnamon and sprinkle over dough. Sprinkle almonds on top. Bake 20–25 minutes or until top is golden brown. Serve warm. Serves approximately 20.

Filled Chocolate Cupcakes

Cupcakes:	Filling:
18-ounce package chocolate cake mix	8 ounces cream cheese, softened
Walnuts, chopped	1 egg plus 1 egg yolk
Powdered sugar	Dash salt
	12 ounces chocolate chips

Preheat oven to 350°F. Mix cake-mix batter according to instructions. Fill cupcake liners ⅓ full. In separate bowl, combine filling ingredients. Drop heaping teaspoon of filling into each cupcake. Sprinkle cupcakes with chopped walnuts and powdered sugar. Bake 20 minutes. Makes 32 cupcakes.

Beverages

When deciding whether to serve alcohol, consider the attitudes of everyone who will be attending your shower. Opinions may vary dramatically. If you decide to serve alcoholic punch, be sure to label it or inform your guests that alcohol is an ingredient. You should also provide a nonalcoholic option, especially if you're not aware of every guest's opinion regarding alcohol. Consider serving decaffeinated coffee, too, since many people avoid caffeine these days.

Frozen Daiquiris

8 cups lemon-lime soda
4 cups light rum
12-ounce can frozen lemonade
　concentrate, thawed
12-ounce can frozen limeade
　concentrate, thawed
6 tablespoons powdered sugar
Filberts (optional)

Mix first 5 ingredients in 1-gallon plastic container. Freeze overnight. Mixture will get slushy but should not freeze completely. Stir before serving and garnish with filberts, if desired. Makes thirty 4-ounce servings. (Daiquiris can also be made without rum.)

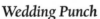

Wedding Punch

Three 12-ounce cans frozen orange
　juice plus 9 cans water
Three 6-ounce cans frozen lemonade
　plus 9 cans water
32-ounce can pineapple juice
1 box frozen strawberries, crushed
1 cup sugar
2 quarts ginger ale

Mix first 5 ingredients well. Set portion of mixture aside to freeze in a mold. (See page 53 to learn how to make an ice ring). Add ginger ale immediately before serving. Makes thirty-five 9-ounce servings.

Serving Suggestions

- When serving large trays of small items on your buffet table, prepare two complete trays of each item. Then as the first tray on the table becomes depleted, the second can be brought out to replace it. This is an especially good idea if items need to be refrigerated.
- Before pouring hot coffee or cold punch into a serving container, temper it with hot or cold water. Not only will this process decrease the chance of breaking a glass pitcher, but your beverages will also stay hot or cold much longer.
- A basket with a handle makes a convenient, attractive breadbasket that can be passed from guest to guest. For a special touch, tie a ribbon around the handle and line the basket with a ruffled cloth.
- Soups can be as plain or fancy as you like, and they need not be difficult to serve. Place a tureen on your table with a ladle and mugs. Set out a bowl of croutons for garnish.

Special Equipment

If you're planning a large affair, you might want to rent or borrow some of the following:

- Card tables and folding chairs
- Punch bowl and cups
- Pitchers
- Coffeemaker
- Large serving trays
- Champagne glasses

Garnishes

A pretty garnish can add a festive touch to any serving tray or punch bowl. Here are a few ideas:

- Float an ice ring in a punch bowl or set it on a platter to keep appetizers cold. To make an ice ring, layer fruits, such as cherries or citrus slices, and water or punch one inch at a time in a ring mold. Freeze each layer before adding the next. By using punch instead of water, you avoid diluting the punch as the ice melts. To remove the ice ring from the mold, place the mold in two inches of warm water until the ring becomes loose. Then carefully flip it over and add the ice ring to the punch.

- Traditional garnishes include carrot curls, sculpted lemons, radish flowers, tomato roses, and scallion brushes. Refer to a cookbook and try to make them if you have time!

- Arrange a circle of shiny green lemon leaves around the edge of an hors d'oeuvres platter. Tuck in a few tiny mums, daisies, and small bunches of green grapes.

Other eye-appealing garnishes include:

- Cherry tomatoes
- Shiny olives
- Avocado slices
- Hard-boiled egg slices
- Baby dill pickles
- Crisp parsley or mint sprigs

- Bunches of watercress
- Pimiento strips
- Lemon, lime, or orange slices
- Cucumber slices
- Paprika (sprinkling)
- Crumbled cooked egg yolk

Buying the Gift

Selecting your gift can be either a pleasure or a headache, depending on how well you know the tastes and needs of the couple. If you know them well, selecting a gift should be no problem. If not, simply ask the bride, groom, or their families about preferences. Find out what the couple needs most and ask about favorite colors and styles.

Many bridal pairs will have their gift preferences registered at a local department or specialty store. If the couple is already registered, pass the gift registry information along to your guests.

Practical Gifts

Here is a list of popular gift ideas. Less expensive items appear first, but keep in mind that brand names and sales can greatly vary the final price of any item.

Kitchen
Potholders
Toaster
Electric knife
Mixing bowls
Glassware
Serving pieces
Mixer
Food processor

Can opener
Napkins/decorative rings
Tablecloth
Storage containers
Dishes
Cutlery
Crock-Pot

Cutting board
Place mats
Bakeware
Coffeemaker/flavored
   coffees
Cookware
Blender

Dining Room
Candlesticks
Tea set
China

Decorative items
Table linens
Crystal stemware

Punch bowl
Silver

Bathroom
Decorative soaps
Towels

Toiletries
Rugs

Washcloths

Bedroom
Breakfast tray
Pillows

Alarm clock
Blankets

Lamp
Sheets

Personal
Sachets
Slippers

Candles
Lingerie/pajamas/robe

Photo frames
Perfume/cologne

Recreation

CDs	Videos	Board games
Cooler	Barware	Tailgating supplies
Card table and chairs	Sporting goods	Luggage

Domestic

Cleaning supplies	Laundry basket	Iron
Organizational items	Power tools	

Handcrafted and Unusual Gifts

You might be tempted to buy a beautifully hand-painted china napkin holder rather than the practical, shatterproof casserole dish listed on the couple's registry. Go ahead and buy it, if you know the couple's tastes and know they're not lacking the essentials. However, newlyweds eating from paper plates with plastic utensils may not appreciate a china napkin holder—unless it appeals to their need for aesthetics in a time of austerity.

Craft fairs and boutiques are good resources for unique gifts. However, before you buy this type of gift, make sure the color, size, and style fit the couple's tastes, since many of these items can't be returned.

Some popular handcrafted gifts include:

- Hand-painted pottery or ceramics
- Frame for a wedding photo or wedding invitation
- Holiday decorations
- Embroidered linen
- Personalized items

Theme Gifts

You'll have a lot of fun selecting the related presents that make up a theme gift, and the bride will have just as much fun opening them, especially if you've wrapped each gift individually to prolong the excitement. Giving a theme gift can be as simple as creatively packaging basic household items (or less practical items, if the bride already has the basics). Consider the following themes:

- Fill a bathroom wastebasket with matching bath accessories, pretty soaps, and coordinated guest towels.
- Fill a pottery jar with assorted kitchen utensils, such as wooden spoons, spatulas, and whisks.
- Assemble several items to be used in an emergency, such as a case of canned goods in the event of a blizzard.
- Fill a brightly colored plastic bucket with an assortment of sponges, polishing cloths, scrub brushes, rubber gloves, and cleaning products. Include a list of your favorite cleaning hints or a book of household hints.
- Fill a laundry basket with detergent, stain remover, fabric softener, spray starch, and a portable drying rack.
- Fill a breadbasket with an assortment of jellies and unusual spreaders.
- Present a chip-and-dip bowl with salsas.

Money Tree

Money is always the right color and never has to be returned. Consider this option if the bride and groom are restoring an old house, or if they're particularly hard to buy gifts for, or if you don't have time to shop.

Make your gift presentation fun by creating a money tree. Stand a tree branch in a large container filled with sand or gravel, or buy a potted indoor tree. (Norfolk pine is a good choice if handled gently.) As guests arrive, give each a clothespin to attach his or her envelope to the tree branches. The same technique could be used with gift certificates.

Gift-Wrapping

- 🎀 Buy some pretty paper, ribbon, and a ready-made bow. Use an inexpensive part of your gift to decorate the package. Wrap your main gift and tie the extra gift to the bow. For example, if your gift is a set of mixing bowls, tie a ribbon around a set of wooden spoons and fasten the unusual bow to the package.
- 🎀 Colorful gift bags are fun, too. Fill a gift bag with colored tissue paper, place your gift inside, and tie your card to the handles.
- 🎀 Make a beautiful tissue paper flower to use for a bow. Cut six to eight layers of tissue paper into 8-by-5-inch rectangles. (Increase the size to make larger bows once you've mastered making the smaller ones.) Use one or more colors of tissue paper to match your package. Accordion-fold the layers of tissue in one-inch folds, then trim them like this: Wrap a pipe cleaner around the center of the folded tissue paper and twist the ends together tightly to cinch the center. Fan out the accordion folds and gently pull out the layers to form "petals."

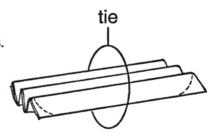

tie

Tip: Ask your guests to write short descriptions of their gifts on the back of gift cards. This will minimize mix-ups and help the person recording the gifts. (Also see the Shower Gift Record on page 62.)

Appendix

Tips for Making Your Own Invitations

- ❧ Make sure you can find envelopes for customized invitations. You may want to select the envelopes first, then create invitations that will fit inside.
- ❧ To save money, create invitation postcards. Write party details on one side of the card, leaving room for mailing information on the other. Select a heavy card stock so the invitations won't be damaged in the mail.
- ❧ Be sure to include all pertinent information on your invitations:
  - ❑ Name(s) of the guest(s) of honor
  - ❑ Date, time, and address of the shower
  - ❑ Your name, address, and telephone number
  - ❑ RSVP information
  - ❑ Theme information
  - ❑ Gift registry information (including the couple's preferred colors)
- ❧ The way you address your invitations will indicate who's invited. If you're throwing a couple's shower and you're inviting couples, include both partners' names on the envelope.

Shower Gift Record

Shower Date _____   Shower Given by _____

Guest   Gift Given

_____   _____

_____   _____

_____   _____

_____   _____

_____   _____

_____   _____

_____   _____

_____   _____

_____   _____

_____   _____

_____   _____

_____   _____

_____   _____

_____   _____

Guest

Gift Given

Keepsake Scrapbook

Shower Date _____ Shower Given by _____

Guest   Advice

_____   _____

_____   _____

_____   _____

_____   _____

_____   _____

_____   _____

_____   _____

_____   _____

_____   _____

_____   _____

_____   _____

_____   _____

_____   _____

Guest   Advice

_____   _____
_____   _____
_____   _____
_____   _____
_____   _____
_____   _____
_____   _____
_____   _____
_____   _____
_____   _____
_____   _____
_____   _____
_____   _____
_____   _____
_____   _____
_____   _____
_____   _____

Traditional Anniversary Gift List

 1 Paper
 2 Cotton
 3 Leather
 4 Books, fruit, or flowers
 5 Wood or clocks
 6 Iron or candy
 7 Copper, bronze, brass, or wool
 8 Electrical appliances
 9 Pottery or willow
10 Tin or aluminum
11 Steel
12 Silk or linen
13 Lace
14 Ivory
15 Crystal
20 China
25 Silver
30 Pearl
35 Jade or coral
40 Ruby
45 Sapphire
50 Gold
55 Emerald
60 Diamond
75 Diamond

Complete the Quotation

Read aloud the first part of each of the following quotations. Have your guests try to complete the phrase with the original language or with a new funny line.

1. What God hath joined,…
   Answer: let no one put asunder.

2. Love me tender, love me sweet,…
   Answer: never let me go.

3. Lucky at cards,…
   Answer: unlucky in love.

4. Love it…
   Answer: or leave it.

5. I got rhythm, I got music, I got my man. …
   Answer: Who could ask for anything more?

6. It's just as easy to marry…
   Answer: a rich man as a poor one.

7. Absence makes…
   Answer: the heart grow fonder.

8. There is only one happiness in life, to love and…
   Answer: be loved.

9. It is better to have loved and lost…
   Answer: than to never have loved at all.

10. All is fair…
    Answer: in love and war.

The Firstborn Profile

As each guest arrives, choose a category below and ask him or her to give you an appropriate word to fill in the blank. Don't let your guests know what their suggestions are being used for. If necessary, create more categories and add them to the form.

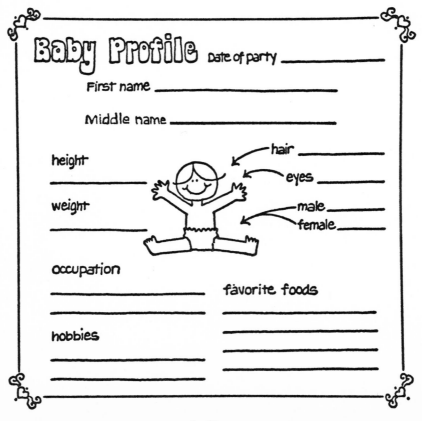

Baby Profile Date of party _____

First name _____

Middle name _____

height
_____

hair _____

eyes _____

weight
_____

male _____
female _____

occupation
_____
_____

favorite foods
_____
_____
_____

hobbies
_____

Notes

Notes

Notes

Notes

Notes

Also from Meadowbrook Press

✦ **The Best Bachelorette Party Book**
This all-inclusive book contains information on how to plan and host a great bachelorette party—plus great games, activities, and recipes. It includes the kind of spicy, fun ideas that bachelorette party-goers are looking for.

✦ **52 Romantic Evenings**
Unlike other romance books that provide only brief outlines of ideas, this book provides everything a couple needs to know to create romantic evenings that will make their relationship come alive. It includes complete plans for a year's worth of romance-filled evenings, detailing where to go, what to wear, what to eat, what to drink, what music to play, and more.

✦ **Create a Date**
Here are 52 ideas for fun, relaxing, romantic, and sexy dates guaranteed to add life to your relationship, emphasizing activities couples can do together, rather than for one another. **Create a Date: Book Two**, features 52 more exciting and relationship-enhancing activities, specially designed to bring partners closer.

✦ **The Best Baby Shower Book**
The number one baby shower planner has been updated for the new millennium. This contemporary guide for planning baby showers is full of helpful hints, recipes, decorating ideas, and activities that are fun without being juvenile.

We offer many more titles written to delight, inform, and entertain.
To order books with a credit card or browse our full
selection of titles, visit our web site at:

www.meadowbrookpress.com

or call toll-free to place an order, request a free catalog, or ask a question:

1-800-338-2232

Meadowbrook Press   •   5451 Smetana Drive   •   Minnetonka, MN   •   55343